Copyright 2020 by James Zamora- All rights reserved.

This document is geared towards providing exact and reliable information in regards to the topic and issue covered. The publication is sold with the idea that the publisher is not required to render accounting, officially permitted, or otherwise, qualified services. If advice is necessary, legal or professional, a practiced individual in the profession should be ordered.

Under no circumstance will any legal responsibility or blame be held against the publisher for any reparation, damages, or monetary loss due to the information herein, either directly or indirectly.

Legal Notice: The book is copyright protected. This is only for personal use. You cannot amend, distribute, sell, use, quote or paraphrase any part or the content within this book without the consent of the author.

Disclaimer Notice: Please note the information contained within this document is for educational and entertainment purposes only. Every attempt has been made to provide accurate, up to date and reliable complete information. No warranties of any kind are expressed or implied. Readers acknowledge that the author is not engaging in the rendering of legal, financial, medical or professional advice. The content of this book has been derived from various sources. Please consult a licensed professional before attempting any techniques outlined in this book.

TABLE OF CONTENTS

Introduction: 6
INSTANT VORTEX V. INSTANT OMNI 7
Breakfast Recipes 8
    Breakfast Oatmeal Cups 8
    Breakfast Potatoes 9
    Baked Almond Butter Oatmeal 10
    Crustless Quiche 11
    Breakfast Cheese Frittata 12
    Simple Cinnamon Baked Oatmeal 13
    Coconut Zucchini Muffins 14
    Mini Egg Muffins 15
    Oatmeal Cake 16
    Mix Veggie Muffins 17
    Broccoli Cheese Muffins 18
    Italian Breakfast Frittata 19
    Easy Broccoli Egg Bake 20
    Berry Oatmeal 21
Poultry Recipes 22
    Cumin Garlic Chicken Wings 22
    Chicken Fajita Casserole 23
    Tasty Chicken Tandoori 24
    Juicy Spicy Chicken Wings 25
    Easy Chili Garlic Chicken Wings 26
    Delicious Fajita Chicken 27
    Thyme Turkey Breast 28
    Chicken Ricotta Meatballs 29
    Easy Turkey Meatballs 30
    Mustard Chicken Tenders 31
    Chicken Meatballs 32
    Cheese Herb Chicken Wings 33
    Garlic Herb Seasoned Chicken Breast 34
    Caribbean Chicken 35
Meat Recipes 36
    Easy Beef Roast 36
    Simple Sirloin Steak 37

Meatballs 38
Quick & Easy Kabab 39
Meatloaf 40
Meatballs 41
Meatloaf 42
Burger Patties 43
Rosemary Dill Beef Roast 44
Meatballs 45
Easy Jerk Pork Butt 46
Quick & Easy Pork Chops 47
Cajun Pork Chops 48
Oregano Lamb Chops 49

Vegetarian Recipes 50
Mac & Cheese 50
Roasted Apple Sweet Potatoes 51
Cheesy Broccoli Casserole 52
Cheesy Broccoli Rice 53
Parmesan Brussels Sprouts 54
Garlicky Cauliflower Florets 55
Flavors Green Beans 56
Potato Casserole 57
Zucchini Egg Bake 58
Broccoli Fritters 59
Balsamic Baked Mushrooms 60
Curried Cauliflower 61
Baked Vegetables 62
Roasted Broccoli Cauliflower 63
Arugula Artichoke Dip 64
Baked Zucchini Eggplant 65

Seafood Recipes 66
Tomato Basil Fish 66
Dijon Maple Salmon 67
Greek Fish 68
Baked Zucchini Cod 69
Lemon Garlic Tilapia 70
Chili Lemon Orange Salmon 71

Mediterranean Salmon 72
Delicious Shrimp Scampi 73
Pesto Salmon 74
Air Fryer Salmon 75
Hot Prawns 76
Tasty Crab Cakes 77
Easy Ginger Garlic Shrimp 78
Simple Salmon Patties 79
Chili Garlic Shrimp 80

Snacks & Appetizers Recipes 81
Buffalo Chicken Dip 81
Artichoke Dip 82
Cheese Stuffed Jalapenos 83
Ranch Chickpeas 84
Cauliflower Hummus 85
Easy Roasted Brussels Sprouts 86
Air Fried Cauliflower Florets 87
Herb Mushrooms 88
Cinnamon Sweet Potato Bites 89
Spicy Mix Nuts 90
Easy Roasted Walnuts 91
Rosemary Cauliflower Bites 92
Sweet Potato Croquettes 93
Sweet & Spicy Mixed Nuts 94
Cheese Dip 95
Creamy Zucchini Dip 96

Desserts Recipes 97
Pear Bread Pudding 97
Egg Soufflé 98
Blueberry Bars 100
Pumpkin Muffins 101
Delicious Strawberry Bars 102
Baked Donuts 103
Eggless Brownies 104
Banana Brownies 105
Yummy Butter Cake 106

Cinnamon Cranberry Muffins 107
Easy Blueberry Cake 108

INTRODUCTION:

Instant Omni Air Fryer Toaster Oven is perfect for home cooks who want fast, nutritious, easy meals every day—at the touch of a button. Its extra-large capacity fits 6 slices of toast or a 12" pizza, and lets you air fry, dehydrate, roast, toast, bake and broil all the food you need to feed your family and your friends.

Quick and even heating ensures crispy, golden results every time. With a variety of one-touch cooking options there's no need to calculate temperature, weight or time. Just select one of the 7 Smart Programs and press start. However, for you foodies out there, the Omni Toaster Oven provides the flexibility to adjust settings to customize your culinary experience. Temperature and Time dials let you let you dial it up, or dial it down to make your food just the way you like it. This air fry toaster oven also comes with all the accessories you need for rotisserie cooking.=

The high performance convection oven, along with the rotisserie function, delivers juicy, delicious rotisserie dishes.

INSTANT VORTEX V. INSTANT OMNI

The Omni is billed as primarily a toaster oven, but it is an excellent air fryer as well and has 7 in 1 features. It is much larger than the Vortex and Vortex Plus and also has a rotisserie, but lacks the rotating rotisserie basket.

Key differences between the Vortex Plus and the Omni are:
- Omni does not have Teflon, Vortex Plus has Teflon.
- Omni lacks a rotating basket, Vortex Plus has the rotating basket.
- Door on Omni does not remove for cleaning but it does have a removable crumb tray.   Vortex Plus has a drip tray and removable door.
- Omni is significantly larger than the Vortex Plus.
- Omni heats to 450, Vortex Plus to 400.
- Omni takes longer to preheat.
- Omni has bottom heating elements for toasting without turning. The Vortex Plus has top only heating.

BREAKFAST RECIPES

BREAKFAST OATMEAL CUPS

Cooking Time: 30 minutes
Serves: 12

Ingredients
- 3 cups old fashioned oats
- 1 1/2 cups unsweetened almond milk
- 1/2 tsp vanilla
- 1 1/2 tsp cinnamon
- 1 cup apples, chopped
- 1/4 cup maple syrup
- 1 1/4 cups unsweetened applesauce
- 1 tsp baking powder
- 1/4 tsp salt

Directions
1. Spray a muffin tray with cooking spray.
2. Add all ingredients except for the apples in a large mixing bowl and mix until well combined. Add apples and fold well.
3. Pour batter into the prepared muffin tray.
4. Select bake mode and set the omni to 350 F for 30 minutes once the oven beeps, place muffin tray into the oven.
5. Serves and enjoy.

BREAKFAST POTATOES

Cooking Time: 35 minutes
Serves: 4

Ingredients
- 2 lbs potatoes, scrubbed and cut into ½-inch cubes
- 1 tbsp olive oil
- 1/2 tsp paprika
- 1 tsp garlic powder
- Pepper
- Salt

Directions
1. Place potato cubes on the parchment-lined cooking pan. Drizzle with oil and season with paprika, garlic powder, pepper, and salt. Toss well.
2. Select bake mode and set the omni to 425 F for 25 minutes once the oven beeps, place the cooking pan into the oven.
3. Toss potatoes and roast for 10-15 minutes more.
4. Allow cooling for 5-10 minutes.
5. Serves and enjoy.

BAKED ALMOND BUTTER OATMEAL

Cooking Time: 35 minutes
Serves: 2

Ingredients
- 2 cups old fashioned oats
- 1/2 cup almond butter
- 1 3/4 cup unsweetened almond milk
- 2 tsp vanilla
- 1/4 cup maple syrup
- 1/4 tsp salt

Directions
1. Spray a baking dish with cooking spray and set aside.
2. In a large mixing bowl, whisk together almond milk, vanilla, maple syrup, almond butter, and salt. Add oats and stir to mix.
3. Pour oats mixture into the prepared baking dish.
4. Select bake mode and set the omni to 375 F for 35 minutes once the oven beeps, place the baking dish into the oven.
5. Serves and enjoy.

CRUSTLESS QUICHE

Cooking Time: 45 minutes
Serves: 6

Ingredients
- 6 eggs
- 1 cup cheddar cheese, grated
- 1 cup tomatoes, chopped
- 1 cup milk
- Pepper
- Salt

Directions
1. Spray an 8-inch pie dish with cooking spray and set aside.
2. In a bowl, whisk eggs with cheese, milk, pepper, and salt. Add tomatoes and stir well.
3. Pour egg mixture into the prepared pie dish.
4. Select bake mode and set the omni to 350 F for 45 minutes once the oven beeps, place the pie dish into the oven.
5. Serves and enjoy.

BREAKFAST CHEESE FRITTATA

Cooking Time: 30 minutes
Serves: 6

Ingredients
- 6 eggs
- 3/4 cup mozzarella cheese
- 1/4 cup fresh basil, chopped
- 1/2 cup tomatoes, chopped
- 2 tbsp water
- Pepper
- Salt

Directions
1. Spray an 8-inch pie dish with cooking spray and set aside.
2. In a bowl, whisk eggs with water, 1/2 cheese, pepper, and salt.
3. Add remaining cheese, basil, and tomatoes and stir well.
4. Pour egg mixture into the prepared pie dish.
5. Select bake mode and set the omni to 350 F for 30 minutes once the oven beeps, place the pie dish into the oven.
6. Serves and enjoy.

SIMPLE CINNAMON BAKED OATMEAL

Cooking Time: 25 minutes
Serves: 6

Ingredients
- 2 eggs, lightly beaten
- 1 1/4 cup milk
- 1/2 cup butter, melted
- 1 cup brown sugar
- 3 cups quick oats
- 1 tsp ground cinnamon
- 1 tsp vanilla
- 1 tbsp baking powder

Directions
1. Spray an 8-inch baking dish with cooking spray.
2. In a bowl, whisk sugar, vanilla, cinnamon, baking powder, eggs, milk, and butter until well combined. Add oats and stir well.
3. Pour oat mixture into the prepared baking dish.
4. Select bake mode and set the omni to 350 F for 25 minutes once the oven beeps, place the baking dish into the oven.
5. Serves and enjoy.

COCONUT ZUCCHINI MUFFINS

Cooking Time: 25 minutes
Serves: 6

Ingredients
- 3 eggs
- 1/4 tsp baking soda
- 1/4 cup Erythritol
- 1/4 cup coconut flour
- 3/4 cup zucchini, shredded and squeeze out all liquid
- 1/2 tsp ground cinnamon
- 2 1/2 tbsp coconut oil, melted
- Pinch of salt

Directions
1. Spray 6 silicone muffin molds with cooking spray.
2. In a bowl, whisk eggs with cinnamon, baking soda, sweetener, coconut flour, coconut oil, and salt.
3. Add zucchini and stir to combine.
4. Pour batter into the silicone muffin molds.
5. Select bake mode and set the omni to 350 F for 25 minutes once the oven beeps, place muffin molds into the oven.
6. Serves and enjoy.

MINI EGG MUFFINS

Cooking Time: 20 minutes
Serves: 9

Ingredients
- 4 eggs
- 1/4 cup Sun-dried tomatoes, chopped
- 1/2 cup Kale, chopped
- ½ cup egg whitesPepper & salt, to taste

Directions
1. Spray muffin pan with cooking spray and set aside.In a mixing bowl, whisk eggs and egg whites.Add sun-dried tomatoes, kale, pepper, and salt and whisk well.Pour egg mixture into the prepared muffin pan
2. Select bake mode and set the omni to 350 F for 20 minutes once the oven beeps, place muffin pan into the oven.
3. Serves and enjoy.

OATMEAL CAKE

Cooking Time: 25 minutes
Serves: 8

Ingredients
- 2 eggs1 cup oats1 apple, peeled & chopped
- 1 tbsp butter3 tbsp yogurt
- 1/2 tsp baking powder1/2 tsp baking soda
- 1 tsp cinnamon1 tsp vanilla
- 3 tbsps honey

Directions
1. Add 3/4 cup oats and remaining ingredients into the blender and blend until smooth.Add remaining oats and mix well.Pour batter into the parchment-lined baking pan.
2. Select bake mode and set the omni to 350 F for 25 minutes once the oven beeps, place baking pan into the oven.
3. Slice and Serves.

MIX VEGGIE MUFFINS

Cooking Time: 22 minutes
Serves: 12

Ingredients
- 12 large eggs1/4 cup parmesan cheese, grated
- 1 cup cheddar cheese, shredded
- 3 tbsp onion, minced1/2 tsp mustard powder
- 1/4 cup milk
- 1 tsp olive oil3 cups mixed vegetables, chopped
- 1/2 tsp pepper
- 1/2 tsp salt

Directions
1. Spray muffin pan with cooking spray and set aside.Heat oil in a pan over medium heat.Add mixed vegetables to the pan and sauté until tender.Remove pan from heat and let it cool.In a mixing bowl, whisk eggs, seasonings, and milk. Add sautéed vegetables, onion, and cheeses and whisk well.Pour egg mixture into the prepared muffin pan
2. Select bake mode and set the omni to 350 F for 22 minutes once the oven beeps, place muffin pan into the oven.
3. Serves and enjoy.

BROCCOLI CHEESE MUFFINS

Cooking Time: 20 minutes
Serves: 8

Ingredients
- 8 eggs
- 3/4 cup mozzarella cheese, shredded
- 2 cups broccoli florets, chopped
- 1 onion, grated1 1/2 cups quinoaPepper & salt, to taste

Directions
1. Spray muffin pan with cooking spray and set aside.In a mixing bowl, mix cooked quinoa, broccoli, cheese, onion, pepper, and salt.In a separate bowl, whisk eggs until light.Pour egg into the egg mixture and mix well.Pour quinoa egg mixture into the prepared muffin pan.
2. Select bake mode and set the omni to 400 F for 20 minutes once the oven beeps, place muffin pan into the oven.
3. Serves and enjoy.

ITALIAN BREAKFAST FRITTATA

Cooking Time: 30 minutes
Serves: 4

Ingredients
- 8 eggs2 zucchini, chopped and cooked
- 1 tbsp fresh parsley, chopped
- 3 tbsps parmesan cheese, grated
- Pepper & salt, to taste

Directions
1. Grease baking dish and set aside.In a mixing bowl, whisk eggs with pepper and salt.Add parsley, cheese, and zucchini and stir well.Pour egg mixture into the prepared baking dish.
2. Select bake mode and set the omni to 350 F for 30 minutes once the oven beeps, place the baking dish into the oven.
3. Serves and enjoy.

EASY BROCCOLI EGG BAKE

Cooking Time: 30 minutes
Serves: 12

Ingredients
- 12 eggs1 onion, diced
- 1 cup milk
- 1 1/2 cups cheddar cheese, shredded
- 2 cups broccoli florets, chopped
- Pepper & salt, to taste

Directions
1. Grease a 9*13-inch baking dish and set aside.In a large bowl, whisk eggs with milk, pepper, and salt. Add cheese, broccoli, and onion and stir well.Pour egg mixture into the prepared baking dish.
2. Select bake mode and set the omni to 390 F for 30 minutes once the oven beeps, place the baking dish into the oven.
3. Serves and enjoy.

BERRY OATMEAL

Cooking Time: 20 minutes
Serves: 4

Ingredients
- 1 egg1/4 cup maple syrup1 1/2 cups milk1 1/2 tsp baking powder2 cups old fashioned oats1 cup blueberries1/2 cup blackberries1/2 cup strawberries, sliced
- 1/2 tsp salt

Directions
1. Grease baking dish and set aside.In a mixing bowl, mix together oats, salt, and baking powder.Add vanilla, egg, maple syrup, and milk and stir well.Add berries and stir well.Pour mixture into the baking dish.
2. Select bake mode and set the omni to 375 F for 20 minutes once the oven beeps, place the baking dish into the oven.
3. Serves and enjoy.

POULTRY RECIPES

CUMIN GARLIC CHICKEN WINGS

Cooking Time: 44 minutes
Serves: 6

Ingredients
- 12 chicken wings
- 3 tbsp ghee
- 1/2 tsp black pepper
- 1/2 tsp turmeric
- 2 tsp cumin seeds
- 2 garlic clove, minced
- 1/2 tsp salt

Directions
1. In a large bowl, mix together 1 teaspoon cumin, 1 tbsp ghee, turmeric, pepper, and salt.
2. Add chicken wings to the bowl and toss until well coated.
3. Spread chicken wings on a cooking pan.
4. Select bake mode and set the omni to 425 F for 30 minutes once the oven beeps, place the cooking pan into the oven.
5. Turn chicken wings to the other side and bake for 8 minutes more.
6. Meanwhile, heat remaining ghee in a pan over medium heat. Add garlic and cumin to the pan and cook for 1 minute. Remove pan from heat and set aside.
7. Remove chicken wings from the oven and spoon ghee mixture over each chicken wing.
8. Bake chicken wings 5 minutes more.
9. Serves and enjoy.

CHICKEN FAJITA CASSEROLE

Cooking Time: 30 minutes
Serves: 4

Ingredients
- 1 lb cooked chicken, shredded
- 7 oz shredded cheese
- 2 tbsp tex-mex seasoning
- 1 onion, sliced
- 1 bell pepper, sliced
- 1/3 cup mayonnaise
- 7 oz cream cheese
- Pepper
- Salt

Directions
1. Spray a baking dish with butter and set aside.
2. Mix all ingredients except 2 oz shredded cheese in a prepared baking dish.
3. Spread remaining cheese on top.Select bake mode and set the omni to 400 F for 15 minutes once the oven beeps, place the baking dish into the oven.
4. Serves and enjoy.

TASTY CHICKEN TANDOORI

Cooking Time: 15 minutes
Serves: 4

Ingredients
- 1 lb chicken tenders, cut in half
- 1 tsp paprika
- 1 tbsp garlic, minced
- 1 tbsp ginger, minced
- 1/4 cup yogurt
- 1 tsp garam masala
- 1 tsp turmeric
- 1 tsp cayenne pepper
- 1/4 cup parsley, chopped
- 1 tsp salt

Directions
1. Add all ingredients into the large bowl and mix well. Place in refrigerator for 30 minutes.
2. Spray air fryer basket with cooking spray.
3. Add marinated chicken into the preheated air fryer basket.
4. Place air fryer basket into the oven and select air fry mode set omni to the 350 F for 15 minutes. Turn chicken after 10 minutes.
5. Serves and enjoy.

JUICY SPICY CHICKEN WINGS

Cooking Time: 25 minutes
Serves: 4

Ingredients
- 2 lbs chicken wings
- 1/2 tsp Worcestershire sauce
- 1/2 tsp Tabasco
- 6 tbsp butter, melted
- 12 oz hot sauce

Directions
1. Spray air fryer basket with cooking spray.
2. Add chicken wings into the air fryer basket.
3. Place air fryer basket into the oven and select air fry mode set omni to the 380 F for 25 minutes. Stir twice.
4. Meanwhile, in a bowl, mix together hot sauce, Worcestershire sauce, and butter. Set aside.
5. Add cooked chicken wings into the sauce bowl and toss well.
6. Serves and enjoy.

EASY CHILI GARLIC CHICKEN WINGS

Cooking Time: 20 minutes
Serves: 4

Ingredients
- 12 chicken wings
- 1 tbsp chili powder
- 1/2 tbsp baking powder
- 1 tsp granulated garlic
- 1/2 tsp sea salt

Directions
1. Add chicken wings into the large bowl and toss with remaining ingredients.
2. Transfer chicken wings into the air fryer basket.
3. Place air fryer basket into the oven and select air fry mode set omni to the 410 F for 20 minutes.
4. Serves and enjoy.

DELICIOUS FAJITA CHICKEN

Cooking Time: 15 minutes
Serves: 4

Ingredients
- 4 chicken breasts, make horizontal cuts on each piece
- 1 bell pepper, sliced
- 2 tbsp fajita seasoning
- 1/2 cup cheddar cheese, shredded
- 1 onion, sliced
- 2 tbsp olive oil

Directions
1. Rub oil and seasoning all over the chicken breast.
2. Place chicken into the air fryer basket and top with bell peppers and onion.
3. Place air fryer basket into the oven and select air fry mode set omni to the 380 F for 15 minutes.
4. Remove chicken and veggies from air fryer and place on foil piece. Top with shredded cheese and Serves.

THYME TURKEY BREAST

Cooking Time: 60 minutes
Serves: 8

Ingredients
- 2 lbs turkey breast
- 1/2 tsp thyme leaves, chopped
- 1 tbsp butter
- 1/4 tsp pepper
- 1/2 tsp sage leaves, chopped
- 1 tsp salt

Directions
1. Rub butter all over the turkey breast and season with pepper, sage, thyme, and salt.
2. Place turkey breast into the air fryer basket.
3. Place air fryer basket into the oven and select air fry mode set omni to the 325 F for 30 minutes.
4. Turn turkey breast to the other side and cook for 30 minutes more.
5. Slice and Serves.

CHICKEN RICOTTA MEATBALLS

Cooking Time: 10 minutes
Serves: 6

Ingredients
- 2 eggs
- 2 lbs ground chicken breast
- 1/4 cup fresh parsley, chopped
- 1/2 cup almond flour
- 1/2 cup ricotta cheese
- 1 tsp pepper
- 2 tsp salt

Directions
1. Spray air fryer basket with cooking spray.
2. Add all ingredients into the large mixing bowl and mix until well combined.
3. Make small balls from meat mixture and place in the air fryer basket.
4. Place ai fryer basket into the oven and select air fry mode set omni to the 380 F for 10 minutes.
5. Serves and enjoy.

EASY TURKEY MEATBALLS

Cooking Time: 12 minutes
Serves: 4

Ingredients
- 1 egg
- 2 tbsp coconut flour
- 1 lb ground turkey
- 1 garlic clove, minced
- 2 green onion, chopped
- 1/4 cup celery, chopped
- 1/4 cup carrots, grated
- Pepper
- Salt

Directions
1. Spray air fryer basket with cooking spray.
2. Add all ingredients into the large bowl and mix until well combined.
3. Make small balls from the meat mixture and place it into the air fryer basket.
4. Place air fryer basket into the oven and select air fry mode set omni to the 400 F for 12 minutes. Turn halfway through.
5. Serves and enjoy.

MUSTARD CHICKEN TENDERS

Cooking Time: 12 minutes
Serves: 4

Ingredients
- 1 lb chicken tenders
- 1 egg, lightly beaten
- 1/2 tsp paprika
- 1 cup pecans, crushed
- 1/4 cup ground mustard
- 1 tsp pepper
- 1 tsp salt

Directions
1. Spray air fryer basket with cooking spray.
2. Add chicken into the large bowl. Season with paprika, pepper, and salt. Add mustard mix well.
3. In another bowl, add egg and whisk well.
4. In a shallow dish, add crushed pecans.
5. Dip chicken into the egg then coats with crushed pecans. Place into the air fryer basket.
6. Place air fryer basket into the oven and select air fry mode set omni to the 350 F for 12 minutes.
7. Serves and enjoy.

CHICKEN MEATBALLS

Cooking Time: 10 minutes
Serves: 4

Ingredients
- 1 lb ground chicken
- 1/4 cup shredded coconut
- 1 tsp sesame oil
- 1 tbsp hoisin sauce
- 1/2 cup fresh cilantro, chopped
- 2 green onions, chopped
- 1 tsp sriracha
- 1 tbsp soy sauce
- Pepper
- Salt

Directions
1. Spray air fryer basket with cooking spray.
2. Add all ingredients into the large mixing bowl and mix until well combined.
3. Make small balls from bowl mixture and place it into the air fryer basket.
4. Place air fryer basket into the oven and select air fry mode set omni to the 350 F for 10 minutes. Turn halfway through.
5. Serves and enjoy.

CHEESE HERB CHICKEN WINGS

Cooking Time: 15 minutes
Serves: 4

Ingredients
- 2 lbs chicken wings
- 1/2 cup parmesan cheese, grated
- 1 tsp herb de Provence
- 1 tsp paprika
- Salt

Directions
1. In a small bowl, mix together cheese, herb de Provence, paprika, and salt.
2. Spray air fryer basket with cooking spray.
3. Coat chicken wings with cheese mixture and place into the air fryer basket.
4. Place air fryer basket into the oven and select air fry mode set omni to the 350 F for 15 minutes. Turn halfway through.
5. Serves and enjoy.

GARLIC HERB SEASONED CHICKEN BREAST

Cooking Time: 15 minutes
Serves: 5

Ingredients
- 2 lbs chicken breasts, skinless and boneless
- 2 tsp garlic herb seasoning
- 1/4 cup yogurt
- 1/4 cup mayonnaise
- 1 tsp onion powder
- 3 garlic cloves, minced
- 1/4 tsp salt

Directions
1. In a small bowl, mix together mayonnaise, seasoning, onion powder, garlic, and yogurt.
2. Brush chicken with mayonnaise mixture and season with salt.
3. Spray air fryer basket with cooking spray.
4. Place chicken into the air fryer basket.
5. Place air fryer basket into the oven and select air fry mode set omni to the 380 F for 15 minutes.
6. Serves and enjoy.

CARIBBEAN CHICKEN

Cooking Time: 10 minutes
Serves: 8

Ingredients
- 3 lbs chicken thigh, skinless and boneless
- 1 tbsp cayenne
- 1 tbsp cinnamon
- 1 tbsp coriander powder
- 3 tbsp coconut oil, melted
- 1/2 tsp ground nutmeg
- 1/2 tsp ground ginger
- Pepper
- Salt

Directions
1. In a small bowl, mix together all ingredients except chicken.
2. Rub bowl mixture all over the chicken.
3. Spray air fryer basket with cooking spray.
4. Place chicken into the air fryer basket.
5. Place air fryer basket into the oven and select air fry mode set omni to the 390 F for 10 minutes.
6. Serves and enjoy.

MEAT RECIPES

EASY BEEF ROAST

Cooking Time: 45 minutes
Serves: 6

Ingredients
- 2 lbs beef roast
- 1 tsp rosemary
- 1 tbsp olive oil
- 1/4 tsp black pepper
- 1 tsp salt

Directions
1. Mix together oil, rosemary, pepper, and salt and rub all over the meat.
2. Place meat on the cooking pan.
3. Place cooking pan into the oven and select air fry mode set omni to the 360 F for 45 minutes.Serves and enjoy.

SIMPLE SIRLOIN STEAK

Cooking Time: 10 minutes
Serves: 2

Ingredients
- 2 sirloin steaks
- 2 tsp olive oil
- 2 tbsp steak seasoning
- Pepper
- Salt

Directions
1. Brush steak with olive oil and season with steak seasoning, pepper, and salt.
2. Spray cooking pan with cooking spray and place steak on cooking pan.
3. Place cooking pan into the oven and select air fry mode set omni to the 350 F for 10 minutes.
4. Slices and Serves.

MEATBALLS

Cooking Time: 20 minutes
Serves: 4

Ingredients
- 1/2 lb ground beef
- 1/2 lb Italian sausage
- 1/2 cup cheddar cheese, shredded
- 1/2 tsp black pepper
- 1/2 tsp garlic powder
- 1/2 tsp onion powder

Directions
1. Spray air fryer basket with cooking spray.
2. Add all ingredients into the large mixing bowl and mix until well combined.
3. Make small balls from meat mixture and place in the air fryer basket.
4. Place air fryer basket into the oven and select air fry mode set omni to the 370 F for 15 minutes. Turn meatballs and cook for 5 minutes more.
5. Serves and enjoy.

QUICK & EASY KABAB

Cooking Time: 10 minutes
Serves: 4

Ingredients
- 1 lb ground beef
- 1/4 cup fresh parsley, chopped
- 1 tbsp vegetable oil
- 2 tbsp kabab spice mix
- 1 tbsp garlic, minced
- 1 tsp salt

Directions
1. Add all ingredients into the mixing bowl and mix until well combined. Place in refrigerator for 30 minutes.
2. Divide mixture into the four equal portions and make sausage shape kabab.
3. Spray air fryer basket with cooking spray.
4. Place kabab into the air fryer basket.
5. Place air fryer basket into the oven and select air fry mode set omni to the 370 F for 10 minutes. Serves and enjoy.

MEATLOAF

Cooking Time: 15 minutes
Serves: 4

Ingredients
- 2 eggs
- 1 lb ground beef
- 1/4 tsp cinnamon
- 1 tsp cayenne
- 1/2 tsp turmeric
- 1 tsp garam masala
- 1/2 tbsp garlic, minced
- 1/2 tbsp ginger, minced
- 1/4 cup fresh cilantro, chopped
- 1 cup onion, diced
- 1 tsp salt

Directions
1. Add all ingredients into the mixing bowl and mix until well combined.
2. Transfer meat mixture into the greased loaf pan.
3. Place the loaf pan into the oven and select air fry mode set omni to the 360 F for 15 minutes.
4. Slice and Serves.

MEATBALLS

Cooking Time: 8 minutes
Serves: 10

Ingredients
- 5.3 oz minced beef
- 2 oz feta cheese, crumbled
- 2 tbsp almond flour
- 1/2 tbsp lemon zest, grated
- 1 tbsp fresh oregano, chopped
- Pepper
- Salt

Directions
1. Add all ingredients into the mixing bowl and mix until well combined.
2. Make small balls from the meat mixture.
3. Place meatballs into the air fryer basket.
4. Place air fryer basket into the oven and select air fry mode set omni to the 390 F for 8 minutes. Serves and enjoy.

MEATLOAF

Cooking Time: 25 minutes
Serves: 4

Ingredients
- 1 lb ground beef
- 2 oz chorizo sausage, chopped
- 3 tbsp almond flour
- 1 egg, lightly beaten
- 2 mushrooms, sliced
- 1 tbsp thyme, chopped
- 1 onion, chopped
- Pepper
- Salt

Directions
1. Add all ingredients into the large bowl and mix until well combined.
2. Transfer bowl mixture into the loaf pan.
3. Place the loaf pan into the oven and select air fry mode set omni to the 390 F for 25 minutes.
4. Slice and Serves.

BURGER PATTIES

Cooking Time: 45 minutes
Serves: 4

Ingredients
- 10.5 oz beef mince
- 1 tsp basil
- 1 tsp mustard
- 1 tsp tomato puree
- 1 tsp garlic puree
- 1 oz cheddar cheese
- 1 tsp mixed herbs
- Pepper
- Salt

Directions
1. Line cooking pan with parchment paper and set aside.
2. Add meat and remaining ingredients into the large bowl and mix until well combined.
3. Make four medium-size patties from meat mixture and place onto the cooking pan.
4. Place cooking pan into the oven and select air fry mode set omni to the 390 F for 25 minutes.
5. Turn patties to the other side and cook at 350 F for 20 minutes more.
6. Serves and enjoy.

ROSEMARY DILL BEEF ROAST

Cooking Time: 45 minutes
Serves: 8

Ingredients
- 2 1/2 lbs beef roast
- 1 tsp rosemary
- 1 tsp dill
- 1/2 tsp black pepper
- 1/2 tsp garlic powder
- 1/2 tsp onion powder
- 2 tbsp olive oil

Directions
1. Mix together black pepper, garlic powder, onion powder, rosemary, dill, and olive oil. Rub all over the beef roast.
2. Place meat on cooking pan
3. Place cooking pan into the oven and select air fry mode set omni to the 360 F for 45 minutes. Serves and enjoy.

MEATBALLS

Cooking Time: 15 minutes
Serves: 6

Ingredients
- 2 eggs
- 30 oz ground beef
- 3 cheese sticks
- 1 tbsp Italian seasoning
- 1/4 cup parmesan cheese, grated
- Pepper
- Salt

Directions
1. Spray air fryer basket with cooking spray.
2. In a bowl, mix together meat, seasoning, parmesan cheese, and egg. Cut cheese sticks into the pieces.
3. Take a handful of meat mixture and place one piece of cheese string inside and give a round ball shape.
4. Place meatballs into the air fryer basket.
5. Place air fryer basket into the oven and select air fry mode set omni to the 375 F for 15 minutes. Serves and enjoy.

EASY JERK PORK BUTT

Cooking Time: 20 minutes
Serves: 4

Ingredients
- 1 1/2 lbs pork butt, chopped into pieces
- 1/4 cup jerk paste

Directions
1. Add meat and jerk paste into the bowl and mix well. Place in refrigerator overnight.
2. Spray cooking pan with cooking spray.
3. Place marinated meat on the cooking pan.
4. Place cooking pan into the oven and select air fry mode set omni to the 390 F for 20 minutes.
5. Serves and enjoy.

QUICK & EASY PORK CHOPS

Cooking Time: 20 minutes
Serves: 2

Ingredients
- 2 pork chops, boneless
- 1 tbsp dash seasoning

Directions
1. Rub seasoning all over the pork chops.
2. Spray cooking pan with cooking spray. Place pork chops on cooking pan.
3. Place cooking pan into the oven and select air fry mode set omni to the 360 F for 20 minutes. Serves and enjoy.

CAJUN PORK CHOPS

Cooking Time: 10 minutes
Serves: 2

Ingredients
- 2 pork chops, boneless
- 1 tsp paprika
- 3 tbsp parmesan cheese, grated
- 1/3 cup almond flour
- 1/2 tsp Cajun seasoning
- 1 tsp herb de Provence

Directions
1. Mix together almond flour, Cajun seasoning, herb de Provence, paprika, and parmesan cheese.
2. Spray both the pork chops with cooking spray.
3. Coat both the pork chops with almond flour mixture and place on cooking pan.
4. Place cooking pan into the oven and select air fry mode set omni to the 350 F for 10 minutes.
5. Serves and enjoy.

OREGANO LAMB CHOPS

Cooking Time: 5 minutes
Serves: 2

Ingredients
- 4 lamb chops
- 1 garlic clove, minced
- 1/2 tbsp fresh oregano, chopped
- 1 1/2 tbsp olive oil
- Pepper
- Salt

Directions
1. Mix together garlic, olive oil, oregano, pepper, and salt and rub over lamb chops.
2. Place lamb chops on the cooking pan.
3. Place cooking pan into the oven and select air fry mode set omni to the 400 F for 5 minutes.
4. Serves and enjoy.

VEGETARIAN RECIPES

MAC & CHEESE

Cooking Time: 20 minutes
Serves: 10

Ingredients
- 1 lb cooked macaroni
- 1/2 cup flour
- 1/2 cup butter
- 1/2 cup breadcrumbs
- 12 oz cheddar cheese, shredded
- 4 1/2 cups unsweetened almond milk
- Pepper
- Salt

Directions
1. Melt butter in a pan over medium heat. Remove pan from heat and slowly add flour, salt, and pepper in melted butter.
2. Add ½ cup milk and stir until well blended. Return to heat and slowly add remaining milk. Add cheese and stir until cheese is melted.
3. Pour over cooked macaroni and stir well. Transfer macaroni in a casserole dish and sprinkle with breadcrumbs.
4. Place casserole dish in omni toaster oven Bakes at 350 F for 15-20 minutes.
5. Serves and enjoy.

ROASTED APPLE SWEET POTATOES

Cooking Time: 30 minutes
Serves: 2

Ingredients
- 2 large sweet potatoes, diced
- 2 tsp cinnamon
- 2 large green apples, diced
- 2 tbsp maple syrup
- 1 tbsp olive oil

Directions
1. In a large bowl, add sweet potatoes, oil, cinnamon, and apples and toss well.
2. Spread sweet potatoes mixture onto the cooking pan.
3. Select bake mode and set the omni to 400 F for 30 minutes once the oven beeps, place the cooking pan into the oven.
4. Drizzle with maple syrup and Serves.

CHEESY BROCCOLI CASSEROLE

Cooking Time: 30 minutes
Serves: 6

Ingredients
- 16 oz frozen broccoli florets, defrosted and drained
- 1/2 tsp onion powder
- 10.5 oz can cream of mushroom soup
- 1 cup cheddar cheese, shredded
- 1/3 cup unsweetened almond milk

For topping:
- 1 tbsp butter, melted
- 1/2 cup cracker crumbs

Directions
1. Add all ingredients except topping ingredients into the casserole dish.
2. In a small bowl, mix together cracker crumbs and melted butter and sprinkle over the casserole dish mixture.
3. Select bake mode and set the omni to 350 F for 30 minutes once the oven beeps, place casserole dish into the oven.
4. Serves and enjoy.

CHEESY BROCCOLI RICE

Cooking Time: 20 minutes
Serves: 8

Ingredients
- 1 1/2 cups cooked brown rice
- 1 garlic clove, chopped
- 16 oz frozen broccoli florets
- 1 large onion, chopped
- 1 tbsp butter
- 3 tbsp parmesan cheese, grated
- 10.5 oz condensed cheddar cheese soup
- 1/3 cup unsweetened almond milk

Directions
1. Heat butter in a pan over medium heat. Add onion and cook until tender.
2. Add garlic and broccoli and cook until broccoli is tender. Stir in rice, soup, and milk and cook until hot.
3. Stir in cheese and pour broccoli mixture into the 11*8*2-inch baking dish.
4. Select bake mode and set the omni to 350 F for 20 minutes once the oven beeps, place the baking dish into the oven.
5. Serves and enjoy.

PARMESAN BRUSSELS SPROUTS

Cooking Time: 12 minutes
Serves: 4

Ingredients
- 1 lb Brussels sprouts, cut stems and halved
- 1 1/2 tbsp olive oil
- 1/4 cup parmesan cheese, grated
- Pepper
- Salt

Directions
1. Toss Brussels sprouts, oil, pepper, and salt into the bowl.
2. Transfer Brussels sprouts into the air fryer basket.
3. Place air fryer basket into the oven and select air fry mode set omni to the 350 F for 12 minutes. Stir twice.
4. Top with parmesan cheese and Serves.

GARLICKY CAULIFLOWER FLORETS

Cooking Time: 20 minutes
Serves: 4

Ingredients
- 5 cups cauliflower florets
- 1/2 tsp cumin powder
- 1/2 tsp coriander powder
- 6 garlic cloves, chopped
- 4 tablespoons olive oil
- 1/2 tsp salt

Directions
1. Add all ingredients into the large bowl and toss well.
2. Add cauliflower florets into the air fryer basket.
3. Place air fryer basket into the oven and select air fry mode set omni to the 400 F for 20 minutes. Stir twice.
4. Serves and enjoy.

FLAVORS GREEN BEANS

Cooking Time: 10 minutes
Serves: 2

Ingredients
- 2 cups green beans
- 1/8 tsp cayenne pepper
- 1/8 tsp ground allspice
- 1/4 tsp ground cinnamon
- 1/2 tsp dried oregano
- 2 tbsp olive oil
- 1/4 tsp ground coriander
- 1/4 tsp ground cumin
- 1/2 tsp salt

Directions
1. Add all ingredients into the mixing bowl and toss well.
2. Spray air fryer basket with cooking spray.
3. Add bowl mixture into the air fryer basket.
4. Place air fryer basket into the oven and select air fry mode set omni to the 370 F for 10 minutes. Serves and enjoy.

POTATO CASSEROLE

Cooking Time: 35 minutes
Serves: 6

Ingredients
- 5 eggs1/2 cup cheddar cheese, shredded
- 2 medium potatoes, diced into 1/2-inch cubes
- 1 green bell pepper, diced
- 1 onion, chopped
- 1 tbsp olive oil
- 3/4 tsp pepper3/4 tsp salt

Directions
1. Spray 9*9-inch casserole dish with cooking spray and set aside.Heat olive oil in a large pan over medium heat.Add onion and sauté for 1 minute. Add potatoes, bell peppers, ½ tsp black pepper, and 1.2 tsp salt and sauté for 4 minutes more or until onions are softened.
2. Transfer sautéed vegetables to the prepared casserole dish and spread evenly.In a bowl, whisk eggs, and remaining pepper and salt.Pour egg mixture into the casserole dish and sprinkle cheddar cheese on top.Select bake mode and set the omni to 350 F for 35 minutes once the oven beeps, place casserole dish into the oven.
3. Serves and enjoy.

ZUCCHINI EGG BAKE

Cooking Time: 30 minutes
Serves: 4

Ingredients
- 6 eggs
- 1/2 tsp dill
- 1/2 tsp oregano
- 1/2 tsp basil
- 1/2 tsp baking powder
- 1/2 cup almond flour
- 1 cup cheddar cheese, shredded
- 1 cup kale, chopped
- 1 onion, chopped
- 1 cup zucchini, shredded and squeezed out all liquid
- 1/2 cup milk
- 1/4 tsp salt

Directions
1. Grease 9*9-inch baking dish and set aside. In a large bowl, whisk eggs with milk. Add remaining ingredients and stir until well combined. Pour egg mixture into the prepared baking dish.
2. Select bake mode and set the omni to 375 F for 30 minutes once the oven beeps, place the baking dish into the oven.
3. Serves and enjoy.

BROCCOLI FRITTERS

Cooking Time: 30 minutes
Serves: 4

Ingredients
- 3 cups broccoli florets, steam & chopped
- 2 cups cheddar cheese, shredded
- 1/4 cup almond flour2 eggs, lightly beaten2 garlic cloves, minced
- Pepper & salt, to taste

Directions
1. Add all ingredients into the large bowl and mix until well combined. Make patties from broccoli mixture and place on a parchment-lined cooking pan.
2. Select bake mode and set the omni to 375 F for 30 minutes once the oven beeps, place the cooking pan into the oven. Turn patties halfway through.
3. Serves and enjoy.

BALSAMIC BAKED MUSHROOMS

Cooking Time: 20 minutes
Serves: 6

Ingredients
- 1 lb button mushrooms, scrubbed and stems trimmed
- 2 tbsp olive oil
- 4 tbsp balsamic vinegar
- 1/2 tsp dried basil
- 1/2 tsp dried oregano
- 3 garlic cloves, crushed
- 1/4 tsp black pepper
- 1 tsp sea salt

Directions
1. Spray a cooking pan with cooking spray and set aside.
2. In a large bowl, whisk together vinegar, basil, oregano, garlic, olive oil, pepper, and salt. Stir in mushrooms and let sit for 15 minutes.
3. Spread mushrooms onto the prepared cooking pan.
4. Select bake mode and set the omni to 425 F for 20 minutes once the oven beeps, place the cooking pan into the oven.
5. Serves and enjoy.

CURRIED CAULIFLOWER

Cooking Time: 15 minutes
Serves: 4

Ingredients
- 2 lbs cauliflower, cut into florets
- 1 1/2 tsp curry powder
- 1 tbsp olive oil
- 1 tbsp cilantro, chopped
- 2 tsp fresh lemon juice
- 1 tsp kosher salt

Directions
1. Toss cauliflower florets in a large bowl with olive oil.
2. Sprinkle cauliflower florets with curry powder and salt.
3. Spread cauliflower florets onto a cooking pan.
4. Select bake mode and set the omni to 425 F for 15 minutes once the oven beeps, place the cooking pan into the oven.
5. Return roasted cauliflower florets into the bowl and toss with cilantro and lemon juice.
6. Serves and enjoy.

BAKED VEGETABLES

Cooking Time: 20 minutes
Serves: 4

Ingredients
- 4 bell peppers
- 2 cups mushrooms
- 1/4 tsp black pepper
- 2 tbsp olive oil
- 2 eggplants
- 1 tsp salt

Directions
1. Cut all vegetables into the small bite-sized pieces and place in a baking dish.
2. Drizzle vegetables with olive oil and season with pepper and salt.
3. Select bake mode and set the omni to 390 F for 20 minutes once the oven beeps, place the baking dish into the oven.
4. Serves and enjoy.

ROASTED BROCCOLI CAULIFLOWER

Cooking Time: 15 minutes
Serves: 12

Ingredients
- 4 cups broccoli florets
- 2/3 cup parmesan cheese, grated and divided
- 4 cups cauliflower florets
- 6 garlic cloves, minced
- 1/3 cup olive oil
- Pepper
- Salt

Directions
1. Preheat the oven to 400 F.
2. Spray a baking dish with cooking spray and set aside.
3. Add cauliflower, broccoli, half cheese, garlic, and olive oil in a bowl and toss well. Season with pepper and salt.
4. Arrange broccoli and cauliflower mixture on a prepared baking dish.
5. Select bake mode and set the omni to 400 F for 15 minutes once the oven beeps, place the baking dish into the oven.
6. Just before serving add remaining cheese and toss well.
7. Serves and enjoy.

ARUGULA ARTICHOKE DIP

Cooking Time: 30 minutes
Serves: 4

Ingredients
- 15 oz artichoke hearts, drained
- 1 tsp Worcestershire sauce
- 3 cups arugula, chopped
- 1 cup cheddar cheese, shredded
- 1 tbsp onion, minced
- 1/2 cup mayonnaise

Directions
1. Add all ingredients into the blender and blend until smooth.
2. Pour artichoke mixture into baking dish.
3. Select bake mode and set the omni to 350 F for 30 minutes once the oven beeps, place the baking dish into the oven.
4. Serves with crackers and enjoy.

BAKED ZUCCHINI EGGPLANT

Cooking Time: 35 minutes
Serves: 6

Ingredients
- 3 medium zucchini, sliced
- 1 medium eggplant, sliced
- 1 tbsp olive oil
- 4 garlic cloves, minced
- 1/4 tsp pepper
- 3 oz parmesan cheese, grated
- 1/4 cup parsley, chopped
- 1/4 cup basil, chopped
- 1 cup cherry tomatoes, halved
- 1/4 tsp salt

Directions
1. Spray baking dish with cooking spray.
2. In a bowl, add cherry tomatoes, eggplant, zucchini, olive oil, garlic, cheese, basil, pepper, and salt toss well until combined.
3. Transfer eggplant mixture into the baking dish.
4. Select bake mode and set the omni to 350 F for 35 minutes once the oven beeps, place the baking dish into the oven.
5. Garnish with parsley and Serves.

SEAFOOD RECIPES

TOMATO BASIL FISH

Cooking Time: 19 minutes
Serves: 2

Ingredients
- 2 cod fillets
- 1 tsp olive oil
- 1 tbsp fresh lemon juice
- 2 tsp parmesan cheese, grated
- 2 tomatoes, sliced
- 1/4 tsp dried basil
- 1/8 tsp pepper
- 1/8 tsp salt

Directions
1. Place fish fillets in greased baking dish.
2. Mix together oil and lemon juice and drizzle over fish fillets. Season fish with basil, pepper, and salt.
3. Arrange tomato slices on top of fish fillets.
4. Sprinkle grated parmesan cheese on top. Cover dish with foil.
5. Select bake mode and set the omni to 400 F for 12 minutes once the oven beeps, place the baking dish into the oven.
6. Serves and enjoy.

DIJON MAPLE SALMON

Cooking Time: 10 minutes
Serves: 6

Ingredients
- 1 lb salmon
- 3 tbsp maple syrup
- 3 tbsp olive oil
- 1 tsp ginger, grated
- 2 1/2 tbsp Dijon mustard
- 1 tsp pepper

Directions
1. In a small bowl, mix together olive oil, mustard, maple syrup, ginger, and pepper.
2. Spray a baking dish with cooking spray and set aside.
3. Place salmon in a baking dish and spread olive oil mixture over salmon evenly.
4. Select bake mode and set the omni to 400 F for 10 minutes once the oven beeps, place the baking dish into the oven.
5. Serves and enjoy.

GREEK FISH

Cooking Time: 15 minutes
Serves: 4

Ingredients
- 4 halibut fish fillets
- 2 tsp olive oil
- 3 tbsp fresh basil, chopped
- 2 tomatoes, chopped
- 2 garlic cloves, minced
- 1 tsp oregano, chopped

Directions
1. Spray a baking dish with cooking spray and set aside.
2. In a bowl, mix together chopped tomatoes, garlic, oregano, and basil.
3. Arrange fish fillets in a baking dish and top with tomato mixture.
4. Select bake mode and set the omni to 350 F for 15 minutes once the oven beeps, place the baking dish into the oven.
5. Serves and enjoy.

BAKED ZUCCHINI COD

Cooking Time: 20 minutes
Serves: 2

Ingredients
- 2 cod fillets
- 1/2 cup olives
- 1/2 cup cherry tomatoes, cut in half
- 1/2 onion, sliced
- 1 cup zucchini, sliced
- 1 red bell pepper, sliced
- 1 tbsp balsamic vinegar
- 3 garlic cloves, minced
- 1 tbsp olive oil
- Pepper
- Salt

Directions
1. Place vegetables in a baking dish. Drizzle with olive oil and season with pepper and salt.
2. Select bake mode and set the omni to 425 F for 10 minutes once the oven beeps, place the baking dish into the oven.
3. Season fish fillets with pepper and salt.
4. Place fish fillets on cooked vegetables and drizzle with vinegar.
5. Bake fish in the oven for 10 minutes.
6. Serves and enjoy.

LEMON GARLIC TILAPIA

Cooking Time: 12 minutes
Serves: 4

Ingredients
- 4 tilapia fillets
- 2 tbsp fresh parsley, chopped
- 1 lemon zest
- 2 tbsp fresh lemon juice
- 3 garlic cloves, minced
- 1/4 cup olive oil
- Pepper
- Salt

Directions
1. Spray a baking dish with cooking spray and set aside.
2. In a small bowl, whisk together olive oil, lemon zest, lemon juice, and garlic.
3. Season fish fillets with pepper and salt and place onto the baking dish.
4. Pour olive oil mixture over fish fillets.
5. Select bake mode and set the omni to 425 F for 12 minutes once the oven beeps, place the baking dish into the oven.
6. Garnish with parsley and Serves.

CHILI LEMON ORANGE SALMON

Cooking Time: 22 minutes
Serves: 4

Ingredients
- 2 lbs salmon fillet, skinless and boneless
- 1/4 cup fresh dill
- 1 chili, sliced
- 2 fresh lemon juice
- 1 orange juice
- 1 tbsp olive oil
- Pepper
- Salt

Directions
1. Place salmon fillet in a baking dish and drizzle with olive oil, lemon juice, and orange juice. Sprinkle chili over the salmon and season with pepper and salt.
2. Select bake mode and set the omni to 350 F for 22 minutes once the oven beeps, place the baking dish into the oven.
3. Garnish with dill and Serves.

MEDITERRANEAN SALMON

Cooking Time: 20 minutes
Serves: 1

Ingredients
- 4 oz salmon fillet
- 1 tbsp fresh parsley, chopped
- 1 tbsp olive oil
- 1 garlic clove, sliced
- 1/4 onion, diced
- 1/2 lemon juice
- 4 grape tomatoes
- Pepper
- Salt

Directions
1. Add all ingredients except lemon juice into the mixing bowl and let sit for 1 hour.
2. Transfer bowl mixture into the baking dish Drizzle with lemon juice. Cover dish with foil.
3. Select bake mode and set the omni to 350 F for 20 minutes once the oven beeps, place the baking dish into the oven.
4. Serves and enjoy.

DELICIOUS SHRIMP SCAMPI

Cooking Time: 13 minutes
Serves: 4

Ingredients
- 1 lb shrimp, peeled and deveined
- 1/4 cup parmesan cheese, grated
- 8 garlic cloves, peeled
- 2 tbsp olive oil
- 1 fresh lemon, cut into wedges

Directions
1. Preheat the oven to 200 C/ 400 F.
2. Add all ingredients except parmesan cheese into the mixing bowl and toss well.
3. Transfer shrimp mixture into the baking dish.
4. Select bake mode and set the omni to 400 F for 13 minutes once the oven beeps, place the baking dish into the oven.
5. Sprinkle with parmesan cheese and Serves.

PESTO SALMON

Cooking Time: 20 minutes
Serves: 2

Ingredients
- 2 salmon fillets
- 1/4 cup parmesan cheese, grated

For pesto:
- 1/4 cup parmesan cheese, grated
- 1/4 cup pine nuts
- 1/4 cup olive oil
- 1 1/2 cups fresh basil leaves
- 2 garlic cloves, peeled and chopped
- 1/2 tsp pepper
- 1/2 tsp salt

Directions
1. Add all pesto ingredients into the food processor and process until smooth.
2. Place salmon fillets in a baking dish and spread 2 tablespoons of the pesto on each salmon fillet.
3. Sprinkle grated cheese on top of the pesto.
4. Select bake mode and set the omni to 400 F for 20 minutes once the oven beeps, place the baking dish into the oven.
5. Serves and enjoy.

AIR FRYER SALMON

Cooking Time: 7 minutes
Serves: 2

Ingredients
- 2 salmon fillets, remove bones
- 2 tsp olive oil
- 2 tsp paprika
- Pepper
- Salt

Directions
1. Rub each salmon fillet with oil, paprika, pepper, and salt.
2. Place salmon fillets in the air fryer basketPlace air fryer basket into the oven and select air fry mode set omni to the 390 F for 7 minutes.
3. Serves and enjoy.

HOT PRAWNS

Cooking Time: 8 minutes
Serves: 2

Ingredients
- 6 prawns
- 1/4 tsp black pepper
- 1/2 tsp chili powder
- 1 tsp chili flakes
- 1/4 tsp salt

Directions
1. In a bowl, mix together spices add prawns to the bowl and toss well with spices.
2. Spray air fryer basket with cooking spray.
3. Transfer prawns to the air fryer basket.
4. Place air fryer basket into the oven and select air fry mode set omni to the 350 F for 8 minutes. Serves and enjoy.

TASTY CRAB CAKES

Cooking Time: 12 minutes
Serves: 2

Ingredients
- 3/4 cup crabmeat, drained
- 1/4 cup breadcrumbs
- 1 1/2 tbsp mayonnaise
- 1 large egg whites
- 2 green onions, chopped
- 1/2 celery rib, chopped
- 1/2 medium sweet red pepper, chopped
- 1/8 tsp salt

Directions
1. Spray air fryer basket with cooking spray.
2. Place bread crumbs in a shallow bowl. In a bowl, add remaining ingredients except for crabmeat and mix well. Gently fold in crabmeat.
3. Drop a tablespoon of crabmeat mixture to the breadcrumbs and slowly coat and shape into patties.
4. Place crab cakes into the air fryer basket.
5. Place air fryer basket into the oven and select air fry mode set omni to the 375 F for 12 minutes. Turn halfway through.
6. Serves and enjoy.

EASY GINGER GARLIC SHRIMP

Cooking Time: 20 minutes
Serves: 4

Ingredients
- 2 eggs
- 1 lb shrimp, peeled and deveined
- 1 tsp garlic powder
- 1 tsp ginger
- 1/2 cup almond flour
- 1 tsp black pepper

Directions
1. Whisk eggs in a bowl with pepper, garlic powder, and ginger.
2. Add almond flour in a shallow dish.
3. Spray air fryer basket with cooking spray.
4. Dip shrimp in egg mixture then coat with almond flour. Place shrimp into the air fryer basket.
5. Place air fryer basket into the oven and select air fry mode set omni to the 350 F for 20 minutes. Stir halfway through.
6. Serves and enjoy.

SIMPLE SALMON PATTIES

Cooking Time: 10 minutes
Serves: 2

Ingredients
- 1 egg
- 14.5 oz salmon
- 1 tsp dill weed
- 1/2 cup almond flour
- 1/4 cup onion, diced

Directions
1. Spray air fryer basket with cooking spray.
2. Add all ingredients into the mixing bowl and mix well.
3. Make patties from bowl mixture and place it into the air fryer basket.
4. Place air fryer basket into the oven and select air fry mode set omni to the 370 F for 10 minutes. Turn patties halfway through.
5. Serves and enjoy.

CHILI GARLIC SHRIMP

Cooking Time: 7
Serves: 4

Ingredients
- 1 lb shrimp, peeled and deveined
- 1 tbsp olive oil
- 1 lemon, sliced
- 1 red chili, sliced
- 1/2 tsp garlic powder
- Pepper
- Salt

Directions
1. Spray air fryer basket with cooking spray.
2. Add all ingredients into the mixing bowl and toss well.
3. Transfer shrimp mixture into the air fryer basket.
4. Place air fryer basket into the oven and select air fry mode set omni to the 400 F for 7 minutes. Stir halfway through.
5. Serves and enjoy.

SNACKS & APPETIZERS RECIPES

BUFFALO CHICKEN DIP

Cooking Time: 10 minutes
Serves: 8

Ingredients
- 2 can chunk chicken, drained
- 2 cups cheddar cheese, shredded
- 1 cup ranch dressing
- 1 package cream cheese
- 3/4 cup hot sauce

Directions
1. Add chicken and hot sauce to the pan and cook for 2 minutes. Add cream and ranch dressing and stir well.
2. Add half cheese and stir until well blended.
3. Transfer chicken mixture to the baking dish and sprinkle the remaining cheese on top.
4. Select bake mode and set the omni to 370 F for 10 minutes once the oven beeps, place the baking dish into the oven.
5. Serves and enjoy.

ARTICHOKE DIP

Cooking Time: 30 minutes
Serves: 8

Ingredients
- 2 cups mayonnaise
- 8 oz parmesan cheese, grated
- 7 oz can green chiles, diced
- 15 oz can artichoke hearts, drained and chopped

Directions
1. Add all ingredients into the mixing bowl and mix until well combined.
2. Pour mixture into the 2-quart baking dish.
3. Select bake mode and set the omni to 325 F for 30 minutes once the oven beeps, place the baking dish into the oven.
4. Serves and enjoy.

CHEESE STUFFED JALAPENOS

Cooking Time: 25 minutes
Serves: 4

Ingredients
- 10 jalapeno peppers, halved, remove seeds & membranes
- 1 tsp onion powder
- 1 tsp garlic powder
- 1 oz cheddar cheese, shredded
- 6 oz cream cheese

Directions
1. Spray cooking pan with cooking spray and set aside.
2. In a small bowl, mix together cream cheese, garlic powder, and onion powder.
3. Stuff cream cheese mixture into each jalapeno halves.
4. Place jalapeno halves onto the prepared cooking pan and top with shredded cheddar cheese.
5. Select bake mode and set the omni to 350 F for 25 minutes once the oven beeps, place the cooking pan into the oven.
6. Serves and enjoy.

RANCH CHICKPEAS

Cooking Time: 12 minutes
Serves: 12

Ingredients
- 15 oz can chickpeas, rinsed, drained, and pat dry
- 2 tbsp ranch seasoning
- 1 tsp olive oil

Directions
1. Line cooking pan with parchment paper and set aside.
2. In a mixing bowl, toss chickpeas with ranch seasoning and oil.
3. Spread chickpeas onto the prepared cooking pan.
4. Place cooking pan into the oven and select air fry mode set omni to the 380 F for 12 minutes. Stir chickpeas twice.
5. Serves and enjoy.

CAULIFLOWER HUMMUS

Cooking Time: 35 minutes
Serves: 8

Ingredients
- 1 cauliflower head, cut into florets
- 3 tbsp olive oil
- 1/2 tsp ground cumin
- 1 tsp garlic, chopped
- 2 tbsp fresh lemon juice
- 1/3 cup tahini
- Pepper
- Salt

Directions
1. Spray cooking pan with cooking spray.
2. Spread cauliflower florets onto the prepared cooking pan.
3. Select bake mode and set the omni to 400 F for 35 minutes once the oven beeps, place the cooking pan into the oven. Turn cauliflower florets halfway through.
4. Transfer cauliflower florets into the food processor along with remaining ingredients and process until smooth.
5. Serves and enjoy.

EASY ROASTED BRUSSELS SPROUTS

Cooking Time: 35 minutes
Serves: 6

Ingredients
- 2 cups Brussels sprouts, halved
- 1/4 tsp garlic powder
- 1/4 cup olive oil
- 1/4 tsp cayenne pepper
- 1/4 tsp salt

Directions
1. Add all ingredients into the large bowl and toss well.
2. Transfer Brussels sprouts on a cooking pan.
3. Select bake mode and set the omni to 400 F for 35 minutes once the oven beeps, place the cooking pan into the oven. Turn halfway through.
4. Serves and enjoy.

AIR FRIED CAULIFLOWER FLORETS

Cooking Time: 15 minutes
Serves: 4

Ingredients
- 1 medium cauliflower head, cut into florets
- 1/2 tsp old bay seasoning
- 1/4 tsp paprika
- 1 tbsp garlic, minced
- 3 tbsp olive oil
- Pepper
- Salt

Directions
1. In a large bowl, toss cauliflower with remaining ingredients.
2. Spread cauliflower florets onto the cooking pan.
3. Place cooking pan into the oven and select air fry mode set omni to the 400 F for 15 minutes. Stir twice.
4. Serves and enjoy.

HERB MUSHROOMS

Cooking Time: 14 minutes
Serves: 4

Ingredients
- 1 lb mushrooms
- 1/2 tsp ground coriander
- 1 tsp rosemary, chopped
- 1 tbsp basil, minced
- 1 garlic clove, minced
- 1/2 tbsp vinegar
- Pepper
- Salt

Directions
1. Add all ingredients into the large bowl and toss well.
2. Spread mushrooms onto the cooking pan.
3. Place cooking pan into the oven and select air fry mode set omni to the 350 F for 14 minutes. Stir halfway through.
4. Serves and enjoy.

CINNAMON SWEET POTATO BITES

Cooking Time: 15 minutes
Serves: 2

Ingredients
- 2 sweet potato, diced into 1-inch cubes
- 1 1/2 tsp cinnamon
- 2 tbsp olive oil
- 2 tbsp honey
- 1 tsp red chili flakes
- 1/2 cup fresh parsley, chopped

Directions
1. Add all ingredients into the bowl and toss well.
2. Spread sweet potato cubes onto the cooking pan.
3. Place cooking pan into the oven and select air fry mode set omni to the 350 F for 15 minutes. Stir halfway through.
4. Serves and enjoy.

SPICY MIX NUTS

Cooking Time: 4 minutes
Serves: 2

Ingredients
- 2 cup mixed nuts
- 1 tsp ground cumin
- 1 tbsp olive oil
- 1 tsp chili powder
- 1 tsp pepper
- 1 tsp salt

Directions
1. Add nuts and remaining ingredients into the mixing bowl and toss well.
2. Spread nuts onto the cooking pan.
3. Place cooking pan into the oven and select air fry mode set omni to the 350 F for 4 minutes. Stir halfway through.
4. Serves and enjoy.

EASY ROASTED WALNUTS

Cooking Time: 5 minutes
Serves: 6

Ingredients
- 2 cups walnuts
- 1/4 tsp chili powder
- 1/8 tsp paprika
- 1 tsp olive oil
- Pepper
- Salt

Directions
1. Add walnuts, chili powder, paprika, oil, pepper, and salt into the bowl and toss well.
2. Spread walnuts onto the cooking pan.
3. Place cooking pan into the oven and select air fry mode set omni to the 320 F for 5 minutes. Serves and enjoy.

ROSEMARY CAULIFLOWER BITES

Cooking Time: 15 minutes
Serves: 4

Ingredients
- 1 lb cauliflower florets
- 1 1/2 tsp garlic powder
- 1 tbsp olive oil
- 1 tsp sesame seeds
- 1 tsp ground coriander
- 1/2 tsp dried rosemary
- Pepper
- Salt

Directions
1. Add cauliflower florets and remaining ingredients into the large bowl and toss well.
2. Spread cauliflower florets onto the cooking pan.
3. Select bake mode and set the omni to 400 F for 15 minutes once the oven beeps, place the cooking pan into the oven.
4. Serves and enjoy.

SWEET POTATO CROQUETTES

Cooking Time: 60 minutes
Serves: 6

Ingredients
- 2 cups cooked quinoa
- 2 tsp Italian seasoning
- 2 cups sweet potatoes, mashed
- 1/4 cup scallions, chopped
- 1/4 cup parsley, chopped
- 1/4 cup flour
- 1 garlic clove, minced
- 1/4 cup celery, diced
- Pepper
- Salt

Directions
1. Spray cooking pan with cooking spray and set aside.
2. Add all ingredients into the large bowl and mix until well combined.
3. Make 1-inch round croquettes from mixture and place on a prepared cooking pan.
4. Select bake mode and set the omni to 375 F for 60 minutes once the oven beeps, place the cooking pan into the oven.
5. Serves and enjoy.

SWEET & SPICY MIXED NUTS

Cooking Time: 20 minutes
Serves: 16

Ingredients
- 4 cups mixed nuts2 tbsp butter1 tbsp maple syrup1 tsp chili powder1 1/2 tsp salt

Directions
1. In a mixing bowl, mix together melted butter, maple syrup, chili powder, and salt.Add mixed nuts and toss to coat.Spread nuts onto the parchment-lined cooking pan
2. Select bake mode and set the omni to 300 F for 20 minutes once the oven beeps, place the cooking pan into the oven.
3. Serves and enjoy.

CHEESE DIP

Cooking Time: 10 minutes
Serves: 4

Ingredients
- 10 oz goat cheese
- 2 tbsp olive oil
- 1/4 cup parmesan cheese
- 2 garlic cloves, minced
- 1/4 tsp sage
- 1/4 tsp thyme
- Pepper
- Salt

Directions
1. Spray a baking dish with cooking spray and set aside.
2. Add all ingredients into the food processor and process until just combined.
3. Pour mixture into the prepared baking dish and spread well.
4. Select bake mode and set the omni to 400 F for 10 minutes once the oven beeps, place the baking dish into the oven.
5. Serves and enjoy.

CREAMY ZUCCHINI DIP

Cooking Time: 15 minutes
Serves: 6

Ingredients
- 1 lb zucchini, grated & squeeze out all liquid
- 1 tbsp lime juice
- 1 tbsp olive oil
- 1 cup heavy cream
- 1 tsp garlic, minced
- 1 tsp dill, chopped
- Pepper
- Salt

Directions
1. Spray a baking dish with cooking spray and set aside.
2. Add all ingredients into the large bowl and mix until well combined.
3. Pour zucchini mixture into the prepared baking dish.
4. Place baking dish into the oven and select air fry mode set omni to the 375 F for 15 minutes. Serves and enjoy.

DESSERTS RECIPES

PEAR BREAD PUDDING

Cooking Time: 44 minutes
Serves: 8

Ingredients

For Bread Pudding:
- 10½ ounces bread, cubed
- ½ cup pear, peeled, cored and chopped
- ½ cup raisins
- ¼ cup almonds, chopped
- 1½ cups milk
- ¾ cup water
- 5 tablespoons maple syrup
- 2 teaspoons ground cinnamon
- 2 teaspoons cornstarch
- 1 teaspoon vanilla extract

For Topping:
- 1 1/3 cups plain flour
- 3/5 cup brown sugar
- 7 tablespoons butter

Directions
1. In a large bowl, mix well bread, apple, raisins, and walnuts.
2. In another bowl, add the remaining pudding ingredients and mix until well combined.
3. Add the milk mixture into bread mixture and mix until well combined.
4. Refrigerate for about 15 minutes, tossing occasionally.
5. For topping: in a bowl, mix together the flour and sugar.
6. With a pastry cutter, cut in the butter until a crumbly mixture form.
7. Place the mixture into 2 baking dishes evenly and spread the topping mixture on top of each.
8. Arrange a sheet pan in the center of Instant Omni Plus Toaster Oven.

9. Place the 1 baking dish over the sheet pan.
10. Select "Air Fry" and then adjust the temperature to 355 degrees F.
11. Set the timer for 22 minutes and press "Start".
12. When the display shows "Turn Food" do nothing.
13. When cooking time is complete, remove the muffin molds from Toaster Oven and place the pan onto a wire rack to cool slightly.
14. Repeat with the remaining baking dish.
15. Serves warm.

EGG SOUFFLÉ

Cooking Time: 30 minutes
Serves: 6

Ingredients
- ¼ cup butter, softened
- ¼ cup all-purpose flour
- ½ cup plus 2 tablespoons sugar, divided
- 1 cup milk
- 3 teaspoons vanilla extract, divided
- 4 egg yolks
- 5 egg whites
- 1 teaspoon cream of tartar
- 2 tablespoons powdered sugar plus extra for dusting

Directions
1. In a bowl, add the butter and flour and mix until a smooth paste forms.
2. In a medium pan, mix together ½ cup of sugar and milk over medium-low heat and cook for about 3 minutes or until the sugar is dissolved, stirring continuously.
3. Add the flour mixture, whisking continuously and simmer for about 3-4 minutes or until mixture becomes thick.
4. Remove from the heat and stir in 1 teaspoon of vanilla extract.
5. Set aside for about 10 minutes to cool.

6. In a bowl, mix together the egg yolks and 1 teaspoon of vanilla extract.
7. Add the egg yolk mixture into milk mixture and mix until well combined.
8. In another bowl, add the egg whites, cream of tartar, remaining sugar, and vanilla extract and whisk until stiff peaks form.
9. Fold the egg white's mixture into milk mixture.
10. Place mixture into th6 greased ramekins evenly and with the back of a spoon, smooth the top surface.
11. Arrange a sheet pan in the center of Instant Omni Plus Toaster Oven.
12. Place the ramekins over the sheet pan.
13. Select "Air Fry" and then adjust the temperature to 330 degrees F.
14. Set the timer for 16 minutes and press "Start".
15. When the display shows "Turn Food" do nothing.
16. When cooking time is complete, remove the muffin molds from Toaster Oven and place the pan onto a wire rack to cool slightly.
17. Sprinkle with the powdered sugar and Serves warm.

BLUEBERRY BARS

Cooking Time: 30 minutes
Serves: 10

Ingredients
- 1 egg
- 1/2 tbsp baking powder
- 1 cup unsweetened almond milk
- 1/4 cup carrot, shredded
- 1/2 tbsp cinnamon
- 1 tsp vanilla
- 1/3 cup Greek yogurt
- 1/3 cup almond flour
- 1/2 cup coconut sugar
- 2 tbsp coconut oil, melted
- 1/3 cup blueberries
- 1/3 cup granola
- 1/2 cup vanilla protein powder
- 1 1/2 cups flour
- Pinch of salt

Directions
1. Grease 9*9 inch baking dish and set aside.
2. In a large mixing bowl, mix together all dry ingredients and flours.
3. In a separate bowl, whisk together egg, vanilla, coconut oil, milk, and yogurt until smooth.
4. Pour wet mixture into the dry mixture and mix well. Stir in carrots, granola, and blueberries.
5. Pour batter in a prepared baking dish and spread evenly.
6. Select bake mode and set the omni to 350 F for 30 minutes once the oven beeps, place the baking dish into the oven.
7. Serves and enjoy.

PUMPKIN MUFFINS

Cooking Time: 35 minutes
Serves: 12

Ingredients
- 2 eggs
- 1/2 cup maple syrup
- 1 tsp pumpkin pie spice
- 1 tsp baking soda
- 2 cups all-purpose flour
- 1/2 cup chocolate chips
- 1 cup can pumpkin
- 1/2 cup olive oil
- 1/2 tsp salt

Directions
1. Line muffin tray with cupcake liners and set aside.
2. In a large bowl, mix together flour, pumpkin pie spice, baking soda, and salt.
3. In a separate bowl, whisk together eggs, pumpkin puree, oil, and maple syrup.
4. Slowly add dry mixture to the wet mixture and mix well. Add chocolate chips and fold well.
5. Pour batter into the prepared muffin tray.
6. Select bake mode and set the omni to 350 F for 35 minutes once the oven beeps, place muffin tray into the oven.
7. Serves and enjoy.

DELICIOUS STRAWBERRY BARS

Cooking Time: 30 minutes
Serves: 16

Ingredients
- 3/4 cup strawberry preServess
- 1 tsp xanthan gum
- 3/4 cup brown sugar
- 1 cup rolled oats
- 1 cup flour, gluten-free
- 1 tsp vanilla
- 10 tbsp butter, melted
- 1 tsp baking soda
- 1/4 tsp salt

Directions
1. Grease 8*8 baking dish and set aside.
2. In a large bowl, whisk together flour, baking soda, xanthan gum, brown sugar, rolled oats, and salt.
3. Add melted butter and vanilla in flour mixture and stir to combine.
4. Set aside 1/3 of the flour mixture. Transfer the remaining mixture to the prepared baking dish and press down with a spatula. Spread strawberry preServess on top.
5. Spread remaining flour mixture over the strawberry layer.
6. Select bake mode and set the omni to 350 F for 30 minutes once the oven beeps, place the baking dish into the oven.
7. Slice and Serves.

BAKED DONUTS

Cooking Time: 15 minutes
Serves: 12

Ingredients
- 2 eggs
- 1 cup all-purpose flour
- 1/2 cup buttermilk
- 1/4 cup vegetable oil
- 1/2 tsp vanilla
- 1 tsp baking powder
- 3/4 cup sugar
- 1/2 tsp salt

Directions
1. Spray donut pan with cooking spray and set aside.
2. In a bowl, mix together oil, vanilla, baking powder, sugar, eggs, buttermilk, and salt until well combined.
3. Stir in flour and mix until smooth.
4. Pour batter into the prepared donut pan.
5. Select bake mode and set the omni to 350 F for 15 minutes once the oven beeps, place donut pan into the oven.
6. Serves and enjoy.

EGGLESS BROWNIES

Cooking Time: 40 minutes
Serves: 8

Ingredients
- 3/4 cup yogurt
- 1 cup all-purpose flour
- 1/2 cup butter, melted
- 1/3 cup cocoa powder
- 2 tsp baking powder
- 1 cup of sugar
- 1/4 cup walnuts, chopped
- 1/2 cup chocolate chips
- 2 tsp vanilla1 tbsp milk
- 1/4 tsp salt

Directions
1. Grease 8*8-inch baking dish and set aside.
2. In a large mixing bowl, sift flour, cocoa powder, baking powder, and salt. Mix well and set aside.
3. In a separate bowl, add butter, vanilla, milk, and yogurt and whisk until well combined.
4. Add flour mixture to the butter mixture and mix until just combined. Fold in walnuts and chocolate chips.
5. Pour batter into the prepared baking dish.
6. Select bake mode and set the omni to 350 F for 40 minutes once the oven beeps, place the baking dish into the oven.
7. Cut into slices and Serves.

BANANA BROWNIES

Cooking Time: 20 minutes
Serves: 12

Ingredients
- 1 egg
- 1 cup all-purpose flour
- 2 medium bananas, mashed
- 4 oz white chocolate
- 1/4 cup butter
- 1 tsp vanilla1/2 cup sugar
- 1/4 tsp salt

Directions
1. Add white chocolate and butter in microwave-safe bowl and microwave for 30 seconds. Stir until melted.
2. Stir in sugar. Add mashed bananas, eggs, vanilla, and salt and mix until combined.
3. Add flour and stir to combine.
4. Pour batter into the greased baking dish.
5. Select bake mode and set the omni to 350 F for 20 minutes once the oven beeps, place the baking dish into the oven.
6. Slice and Serves.

YUMMY BUTTER CAKE

Cooking Time: 30 minutes
Serves: 9

Ingredients
- 1 egg, beaten
- 3/4 cup sugar
- 1/2 cup butter, softened
- 1 cup all-purpose flour
- 1/2 tsp vanilla

Directions
1. In a mixing bowl, mix together sugar and butter.
2. Add egg, flour, and vanilla and mix until combined.
3. Pour batter into an 8*8-inch greased baking pan.
4. Select bake mode and set the omni to 350 F for 30 minutes once the oven beeps, place baking pan into the oven.
5. Slice and Serves.

CINNAMON CRANBERRY MUFFINS

Cooking Time: 30 minutes
Serves: 6

Ingredients
- 2 eggs
- 1/2 cup cranberries
- 1/4 tsp cinnamon
- 1 tsp vanilla
- 1/4 cup sour cream
- 1 tsp baking powder
- 1/4 cup Swerve
- 1 1/2 cups almond flour
- Pinch of salt

Directions
1. Line muffin tray with cupcake liners and set aside.
2. In a bowl, beat sour cream, vanilla, and eggs.
3. Add remaining ingredients except for cranberries and beat until smooth.
4. Add cranberries and fold well. Pour batter into the prepared muffin tray.
5. Select bake mode and set the omni to 325 F for 30 minutes once the oven beeps, place muffin tray into the oven.
6. Serves and enjoy.

EASY BLUEBERRY CAKE

Cooking Time: 45 minutes
Serves: 8

Ingredients
- 1 egg
- 2 cups blueberries
- 1/2 cup butter, melted
- 2 cups all-purpose flour
- 1/2 cup milk
- 2 tsp baking powder
- 1/3 cup sugar
- Pinch of salt

Directions
1. Grease 8-inch baking dish and set aside.
2. In a large bowl, mix together all-purpose flour, baking powder, sugar, and salt.
3. In a separate bowl, whisk egg, butter, and milk.
4. Add flour mixture into the egg mixture and mix until combined.
5. Pour batter into the prepared baking dish. Spread blueberries on top.
6. Select bake mode and set the omni to 350 F for 45 minutes once the oven beeps, place the baking dish into the oven.
7. Serves and enjoy.